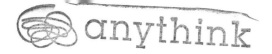

TOOLS FOR CAREGIVERS

- **ATOS:** 0.6
- **GRL:** C
- **WORD COUNT:** 41

- **CURRICULUM CONNECTIONS:** animals, habitats

Skills to Teach

- **HIGH-FREQUENCY WORDS:** a, and, are, has, is, it, look, on, see, they
- **CONTENT WORDS:** away, black, eats, flippers, fur, grows, harp, ice, keeps, lives, pups, seal, snow, spots, swims, up, warm, whiskers, white
- **PUNCTUATION:** exclamation points, periods, question marks
- **WORD STUDY:** long /a/, spelled ay (away); long /e/, spelled ea (eats, seal); long /e/, spelled ee (keeps, see); long /o/, spelled ow (grows, snow); /oo/, spelled oo (look); short /u/, spelled u (pup)
- **TEXT TYPE:** information report

Before Reading Activities

- Read the title and give a simple statement of the main idea.
- Have students "walk" though the book and talk about what they see in the pictures.
- Introduce new vocabulary by having students predict the first letter and locate the word in the text.
- Discuss any unfamiliar concepts that are in the text.

After Reading Activities

Polar babies, like harp seals, live where it is very cold. White fur keeps them warm and helps them blend in with the snow and ice. When they grow older, their fur starts to grow spots. How do readers think this helps them blend in with water while swimming? What other features do seals have that help them swim?

Tadpole Books are published by Jump!, 5357 Penn Avenue South, Minneapolis, MN 55419, www.jumplibrary.com

Editor: Jenna Trnka **Designer:** Anna Peterson

Photo Credits: Eric Baccega/Age Fotostock, cover; Vladimir Melnik/Dreamstime, 1, 10–11; KeithSzafranski/iStock, 2ml, 3; Ingo Arndt/Age Fotostock, 2mr, 4–5; Tom Brakefield/Getty, 2tr, 6–7; M. Watson/ardea.c/Age Fotostock, 2br, 8–9; Biosphoto/SuperStock, 2bl, 12–13; Doug Allan/Getty, 2tl, 14–15; J & C Sohns/Age Fotostock, 16.

Library of Congress Cataloging-in-Publication Data
Names: Nilsen, Genevieve, author.
Title: Harp seal pups / by Genevieve Nilsen.
Description: Tadpole edition. | Minneapolis, MN: Jump!, Inc., (2020) | Series: Polar babies | Audience: Age 3–6.
Includes index. Identifiers: LCCN 2018049325 (print) | LCCN 2018050483 (ebook) | ISBN 9781641287524 (ebook)
ISBN 9781641287500 (hardcover : alk. paper) | ISBN 9781641287517 (paperback)
Subjects: LCSH: Harp seal—Infancy—Juvenile literature.
Classification: LCC QL737.P64 (ebook) | LCC QL737.P64 N55 2020 (print) | DDC 599.79/291392—dc23
LC record available at https://lccn.loc.gov/2018049325

HARP SEAL PUPS

by Genevieve Nilsen

TABLE OF CONTENTS

tadpole
books

WORDS TO KNOW

flippers

fur

pup

snow

spots

whiskers

HARP SEAL PUPS

**Look!
A harp seal pup.**

snow

ice

It lives on snow and ice.

Fur keeps it warm.

fur

It is white.

whisker

It has whiskers.

They are black.

It eats.

spot

It grows up!

See its spots?

flippers

See its flippers?

It swims away!

LET'S REVIEW!

Harp seal pups are white. What else is white where they live?

INDEX